A History and Genealogy

OF THE

Stoakes Family

Which Was Founded in America in the Year
1797--'99

BY

WM. STOAKES SR. and WIFE
ANN HALL STOAKES
Of London, England

John Stoakes

Jane VanTilburg Stoakes

THIS HISTORY AND GENEALOGY

is Dedicated to

GEORGE W. STOAKES

of Traer, Iowa

Only Living Son of John Stoakes Sr.

and

KEZIAH J. HUTCHINSON

of Toronto, Ohio

Oldest Living Descendant of William Stoakes Jr.

———

Author of History
J. S. Hopkins, of Bradgate. Iowa.

———

Compilers of Data for Genealogy
Arthur H. Thomas, of Traer, Iowa
and
J. S. Hopkins, of Bradgate, Iowa

———

Published by Samuel T. Hopkins, of Vancouver, Washington
Press of the Vancouver Daily Columbian

iv

Preface

Almost 100 years ago, Mr. J.S. Hopkins and Art Thomas compiled a book on Stoakes history titled *A History and Genealogy of the Stoakes Family founded in America in the Year 1797 – 1799 by Wm Stoakes Sr. and Wife Ann Hall Stoakes of London, England.* As far as I can tell, it was published around May 19, 1921. This is the date of the birth of triplets in the family, which just made it before publishing. Considering the tools he had to work with, it is a very impressive work. The Stoakes history goes back to the 1700s, includes many children of the two brothers who were sons of William and Ann Hall Stoakes, and takes on the difficult task of distinguishing all of the Williams, Johns, and Sarahs in the Stoakes family. I felt this needed to be made available to the Stoakes descendants.

This book was simply scanned and made into a pdf file. Thanks to Taylor Kvidera for doing this. You will see some handwritten corrections and updates. I'm sure there are other misspellings, incorrect dates, etc. This is meant to be a starting point for genealogical research for the Stoakes family. Thanks also to Clark Kenyon for helping to publish this book. Your talents are greatly appreciated.

I hope to update this family history and have undertaken documenting the additional last 100 years of the Eleazer Stoakes branch of the family tree. I you would like to be included in this upcoming document, please contact me.

Sharon Stoakes
2970 150th Street
Traer, Iowa 50675
Ph. 319.478.2574.
Email: redhawk8223@yahoo.com

Table of Contents

PREFACE TO THE STOAKES FAMILY HISTORY.

A HISTORY of the Stoakes family, was first suggested by relatives to the author while visiting at Traer, Iowa, in the spring of 1919. While considering the matter we were informed that a cousin, Arthur H. Thomas, of Traer, had entertained the idea of a family tree of the John Stoakes, Sr. branch of the family, and had collected considerable data for that purpose, but on account of his professional duties, and the difficulty of collecting full data of so large and widely scattered family, had not completed the undertaking. The writer interviewed him, and it was agreed between us that he would turn over his incomplete data as a foundation for a complete genealogy, and further agreed that the History and Genealogy should be extended to include the William Stoakes, Jr., branch of the family, thus making a complete record of the Stoakes family, which was founded in America by William Stoakes Sr., and his wife, Ann Hall Stoakes, in the later part of the 18th century. This History and Genealogy are the result. In its preparation we have been assisted by many members of both branches of the family. Those who have lent valuable assistance in the collection of Historical and Genealogical data are: John R. Stoakes and daughter, Mary J. Stoakes, of Wellsville, Ohio; George W. Stoakes and wife and Arthur H. Thomas, of Traer, Iowa; and Mrs. Mary E. Kennedy, of Weir, Kansas, on the part of the John Stoakes Sr. branch. On the part of the William Stoakes Jr. branch, we have been assisted by Mrs Keziah J. Hutchinson, of Toronto, Ohio; Miss Ella H. Stoakes, of Oskaloosa, Iowa, who is one of the faculty of Penn College; Mrs. Jessie Young Smith of Uhrichsville, Ohio; and Mrs. Flora V. Rider, of San Leandro, California; all grand-daughters of William Stoakes Jr. We are also indebted to Miss Ella H. Stoakes for extracts from an early pioneer history, "The Morris-Miller History," which was revised and printed by her brother, Frank Stoakes, when a boy of sixteen. This history furnishes many details and reminiscences of the early pioneer life of the Stoakes families, and we append a short supplement. We have also added a short supplement for the Vantilburg family, who were very early pioneers and closely allied by marriage to the Stoakes families. The data for this interesting supplement has been furnished principally by Miss Ella H. Stoakes, Mrs. Flora V. Rider and Mrs. Keziah J. Hutchinson.

In addition to all descendants bearing the Stoakes name, we have included all of the principal branch families; To wit: The Watt and Young families of the William Stoakes Jr. branch, and the Gaston, Hopkins, Rider and Thomas families, of the John Stoakes Sr. branch. We have also included as far as possible the names of the husbands and wives, who have married persons of Stoakes descent.

.With apologies for any slight errors which may have occurred in this work, we assure the relatives and members of this wonderful family, which has done so much for the advancement of our country, of an honest effort and much labor to present an accurate History and Genealogy.

Respectfully,

J. S. HOPKINS,
ARTHUR H. THOMAS.

Note: In the Genealogy of the two families, where there is a repetition of names, we have endeavored to distinguish between the two branches by the use of Roman numerals (I), (II), etc., for the William Stoakes Jr. branch, and Arabic numerals (1), (2), etc., for the John Stoakes Sr. descendants.

A HISTORY OF THE STOAKES FAMILY WHICH WAS FOUNDED IN AMERICA BY WILLIAM STOAKES SR., NEAR THE CLOSE OF THE EIGHTEENTH CENTURY, BETWEEN 1797 AND 1799.

William Stoakes Sr., the founder of the Stoakes family in America, was a retired merchant of London, England, who decided to try his fortune in the New World, and accordingly, anticipating Horace Greeley's advice, "Go West, Young Man," bade farewell to his native land, crossed the Atlantic, and landed at Philadelphia, Pa., and wending his way Westward, making a few stops with parties in Pennsylvania, to whom he had letters of introduction by friends in England, decided on a location in the wilderness of Eastern Ohio, which was then a territory, and took up a tract of land near what is now the town of Knoxville, in Jefferson county. Here he built a log cabin and cleared a small piece of land, which was the beginning of a large farm. Mr. Stoakes was a man of splendid physique and well fitted to endure the hardships of pioneer life. The country was heavily timbered and wild game was plentiful, which contributed largely to the bill of fare of the early settlers. Even panthers were met with occasionally and Mr. Stoakes had the unpleasant experience of being followed by one when returning from a neighbor's who lived several miles distant from his cabin, where he had been to get his laundry. At one time it became very bold and threatening and approached quite near him. Not being armed, he resorted to strategy by taking a white shirt from his bundle and taking a sleeve in each hand, threw it above his head, at the same time giving a loud yell. This had the desired effect, and the panther sprang up the hillside and kept at a safe distance afterward. However, it followed him home and prowled around his cabin the entire night, but had disappeared when daylight came.

Mr. Stoakes spent some time making improvements on his claim, and in about two years sent for his family, which consisted of his wife, Ann Hall Stoakes, two sons, William, aged nine years, and John, aged seven, also a daughter, Sarah, age unknown. They crossed the ocean in a sailing vessel (this was many years before a steam propelled ship had crossed the ocean) and landed at Philadelphia, Pa., having been three months on the ocean. The family remained three months in Philadelphia before the father came and had almost despaired of his coming. He finally arrived, having walked the entire distance of about three hundred miles from his claim. He wore a broad brim hat and was clad in frontier garb, quite a morphosis from the fashionably garbed London merchant. So great was the change that his wife and children scarcely knew him at first sight.

Mr. Stoakes at once went to work to improvise some conveyance to get his family to their future home in the wilds of Ohio. He was resourceful, and purchased an outfit composed of a horse and side saddle, on which Mrs. Stoakes rode, the boys riding alternately behind her (the daughter had died during their stay in Philadelphia) and the father leading the horse. In this way they traveled across the country to Pittsburg, Pa., at the head of the Ohio river. Here his resourcefulness was again tested, but he was equal to the emergency, and constructed a raft on which they floated down the Ohio river about eighty miles, to a point eleven miles from their cabin, and thus they reached their new home.

We leave the reader to draw on his imagination for the contrast between the busy streets of London and this cabin home and surroundings in the dense forests of the frontier. To such brave and heroic men and women, who sacrificed the comforts and privileges of civilization for the pioneer life and its hardships, we owe the foundation of our great country which now stands foremost among the nations of the world. Poets will sing their praises and historians will laud their enterprise and bravery to the end of time.

As far as the writer has been able to learn the settlers of this locality were not troubled by Indians, either hostile or peaceably inclined. We account for this by the fact that it was about the time of, or a few years after, General Wayne's treaty of peace with the savages in 1795, which was immediately after his decisive defeat of the hostile tribes of western Ohio, Indiana and Michigan, and was followed by many years of peace for the pioneers of that section.

The Stoakes brothers grew to manhood, in the meantime assisting in clearing up and improving the large tract of land taken up by their father. They had limited opportunity in the line of education, as the educational facilities were very primitive in their pioneer community. There is a tradition that William Jr. attended one winter term in Pennsylvania, making his boarding place

with Isaac Morris, a friend of his father. They doubtless had
considerable home education, as their parents were well educated
people. Both were largely self educated men and were leading
and influential citizens in the communities in which they lived.
John, grandfather of the writer, took great interest in public affairs, was a strong Whig and great admirer of Henry Clay.

When the "War of 1812" broke out they both joined the
American army. William raised a company and went as captain
and John enlisted as a private soldier. They served under General Harrison on the northwestern frontier until the close of the
war. They were in the "Battle of the Thames", in which the
British and Indians under General Proctor and the great chief,
Tecumseh, were decisively defeated by the American army and
Tecumseh was killed. This great victory broke the British and
Indian power in the northwest. William Stoakes was promoted
to the office of Major and at one time was a member of a select
company which General Harrison organized to capture and burn
several British ships which were icebound not far from Detroit,
but a high wind came up the night before the attack was to be
made and broke up the ice so that the ships escaped. It was
charged by the Americans that General Proctor had promised the
Indians, who outnumbered the British two to one, that if they
would fight bravely and help the British to defeat and capture the
Americans, that the prisoners would be turned over to them to be
dealt with as they saw fit, which meant that they would be tor-
tured and murdered. These Indians entertained a bitter hatred
of General Harrison, who had defeated them only a few years be-
for at the "Battle of Tippecanoe", and would doubtless have shown
no quarter. "Tippecanoe", however, had made different arrange-
ments. At the close of the war the militia were discharged with-
out any provision for transportation to their homes and the
Stoakes brothers with many others were obliged to walk through
the almost roadless wilderness to their homes which were several
hundred miles distant, the best walkers getting home first.

After their return from the war the brothers assisted their
father in clearing the land and making improvements. Soon after
returning from the army William Jr. married Keziah Vantilburg,
and a few years later, in 1818, John married a younger sister, Jane
Vantilburg. The sisters were of a family who located in Jefferson county, near Port Homer, only a few years after the Stoakes
family had settled a short distance further north. William and
Keziah made their home with his parents until their death about

twenty years later, in 1831, and inherited the homestead. They
raised a family of nine children. They lived in the log cabin until about 1825, when they built a fine brick house about half a mile
south of Knoxville, on the Steubenville and New Lisbon road.
Here they lived for many years, until death removed them from
earthly scenes, she dying in 1849 and he in 1859. The homestead
descended to their heirs and is still owned by their descendants.

John and Jane, after their marriage, located on the north
part of the farm, near Yellow Creek, where they lived nearly
thirty years and raised a family of ten children. We have no
data as to what kind of a house they built on the Yellow Creek
farm, but about eight years after their marriage they built a fine
brick mansion, the ruins of which are still standing. A few years
later he built a mill on Town Fork, a branch of Yellow Creek,
where he ground grists for settlers for many miles around. In
1848 he moved to Wellsville, Columbiana county, Ohio, where he
engaged for a few years in the wholesale grocery business, with his
son, Henry, and his son-in-law, J. P. Hopkins for partners. In
1851, he and the oldest son, William, and the unmarried members
of his family moved to VanBuren county, Iowa, where they engaged in farming. In 1855 the whole family moved to Tama county,
Iowa, near the location of the present town of Traer, where they
bought prairie land and opened up farms. Here they lived the
balance of their lives. Mrs. Stoakes died in 1875 and Mr. Stoakes
in 1879, both living to a ripe old age.

The lives of the Stoakes brothers, William Jr., and John Sr.,
came nearer to being on parallel lines than any two persons that
we ever heard of. Besides being children of the same parents,
they were born in the same city and country, crossed the ocean in
the same ship, traveling together to reach their pioneer home,
shared the hardships of frontier life, grew to manhood together,
then served in the same army, and after returning, married sisters, which made their children of the same blood, and finally
settled on adjoining farms and lived for thirty years as neigh-
bors. In a life of nearly eighty years, the writer has never known
of a parallel.

Note: The original Stoakes family were English Quakers,
but we have no reason to believe that it was for religious reasons
that they came to America.

SUPPLEMENT TO THE STOAKES FAMILY HISTORY.

Chapter from the book entitled "A Short Historical Account of the Miller and Morris Families," by Morris Miller.

THE FIRST ACQUAINTANCE OF WILLIAM STOAKES.

About the year 1797 a man in London by the name of William Stoakes, a particular acquaintance of Benjamin West, wished to emigrate to America and requested West to give him a letter of introduction to some of his relatives in Pennsylvania. Stoakes' plan was to come over himself and leave his wife and children until he made a purchase and some improvements and then to send for them. West, having full confidence in the energy and honesty of his friend, gave him a letter of introduction to his brother, Samuel West, who then resided near the old partition of their father. Stoakes arrived with the letter and was kindly received by Samuel, who was always pleased to hear so directly from his brother.

After considering Stoakes' object in all of its bearings they concluded that he had better go west and locate, as the Territory of Ohio was then opening to settlers. Samuel advised him to take a letter of recommendation to his nephew, Isaac Morris, in western Pennsylvania, who being a farmer and having resided there for ten or twelve years he though would be the most suitable person to assist him in selecting a location. Stoakes took the letter and wended his way over the mountains on foot until he came to the residence of Isaac Morris. It being autumn and the roads good he got along very comfortably in his long walk.

As he was an entire stranger he presented the letter to Isaac Morris, who not being educated to read requested Stoakes to read it for him. On hearing its contents he gave Stoakes a very hearty greeting. Isaac was so glad to hear from his old uncle that he lost no time in testing the stranger's sincerity. Though he could not read by letters he was skilled in reading a stranger through as quickly and correctly as those skilled in the rudiments of a high education.

As the shades of evening were drawing on soon Isaac wished to be excused for a little time to attend to some fires in the field below the house before night came. "May I go along?" asked Stoakes. "Oh no," was the reply. "Thee must be weary from thy long journey and perhaps hungry. I will be back soon and we will have some supper."

"Nay," said he, "I am not much tired and would like to go along." Isaac consented and off they went. In taking the deadened timber off the field which he was clearing Isaac had planned it so that each log should burn off the stump, and thus leave the ground entirely free from stumps, hence more attention was necessary than for common log heaps. Soon they returned to the house and enjoyed the evening with much satisfaction as their little work had rendered them very social. Isaac was an early riser and next morning while watching for the first break of day he observed an unusual light beaming through is chamber window. Rising to learn the cause he beheld his fires in the field glowing brilliantly for Stoakes had risen quietly and had the fires in elegant trim. When asked why he had taken so much trouble he said. "I expect to settle in the woods and I want to learn all I can." That circumstance established a friendship between the two men that no deed or event was allowed to interrupt. Isaac proposed to his guest that if he would, as soon as he could, put his farm work in shape to leave, go over to Ohio where they could probably make the most judicious selection, as a land office had recently been opened in the then small village of Steubenville. They crossed the river near that place and selected and purchased a tract of land about eleven miles north of Steubenville in Knox Township, a little south of Knoxville.

Whether Stoakes remained there at that time to build his camp and commence improvement I cannot say but the current impression is that he did, and after about a year went east to meet his wife and children and to conduct them to his intended habitation.

(References in other chapters of the same book.)

The author states that his grandfather, Isaac Morris, wishing to see where his sons were going to locate in Columbiana County and also to visit his friend Stoakes in Jefferson County, went first to the home of the latter who accompanied him on his journey. Stoakes had returned from the east with his wife and two sons, William and John, aged respectively seven and nine, in the autumn of 1799. They sojourned with Isaac Morris a few days and then journeyed on to their new home in Ohio where by persevering industry they had cleared out a farm, planted an orchard, and elevated themselves from their first rustic log cabin to a comfortable hewed log house situated on the public road running from Steubenville to New Lisbon. Thus it was frequently the recipient of many of the first settlers of Columbiana County in passing to and from the land office in Steubenville, as in those days public houses were few and far between, hence the name of William Stoakes was known to many in Columbiana County. The author indicates that Stoakes and Morris frequently visited each other probably almost every year for more than twenty years and that Morris' friends always found a welcome with Stoakes. In 1804-1805 Stoakes' eldest son, William, visited Isaac Morris and attended school one term.

In 1812, during a panic among the Columbiana County settlers because of a false rumor that the Indians were on the war path the father of Morris Miller and his family with many others fled from their homes. Two of the families decided to go to William Stoakes. They rested awhile at the salt works on Yellow Creek and at midnight started on their journey again reaching the home of their friend, Stoakes, about daylight, where they were kindly received and their necessities relieved. In the author's own words: "That day was to be remembered with them as well as ourselves. Their elder son, William, was a captain of a military company and that day they were to rendezvous at his father's house and commence their march for the frontier, their provision and baggage wagon having been prepared the day before."

It is then related that the company assembled at the appointed time, and that their captain took them through a short drill and then addressed them in a brief but very appropriate speech, standing on his father's door step. A little later Henry Boyles with his rifle company, arrived and all marched off towards Steubenville. Recruiting was in progress everywhere at this time. When Morris Miller and his father visited the Stoakes home the next year they found that the younger son had been called into service about a month later than his brother. In order to comfort the lonely old people Isaac Morris sent an eleven year old son, Mordecai, to live with them and do chores during the winter.

Later the author tells of the generosity of William Stoakes, Sr., toward a son-in-law of Isaac Morris in going with him to purchase some land and advancing the money to pay for it, which the purchaser was not able to do for some time, and other prospective buyers were seeking it.   He says, "This I record as one of Stoakes' generous acts."

Again he tells of Stoakes, who had a large crop of fruit, sending an invitation to three of the families of new settlers to come and get all they wanted.   They accepted the invitation and took home three loads of peaches.

A VANTILBURG SUPPLEMENT TO THE STOAKES FAMILY HISTORY.

By J. S. HOPKINS.

The Vantilburg family, which was closely allied to the Stoakes family by marriage, was founded in America by five brothers, who came over from Holland about the year 1770. They came from the province or town of Tilbury, and settled first in New Holland (New York), but three of them, Henry, John and William, crossed over to New Jersey and enlisted in the Revolutionary army under Washington, and were in the battles of Monmouth and Trenton. Henry, who was an artilleryman, had a sad experience in his family while in the army. While standing in the door of her home near Trenton with a babe in her arms, his wife was shot and killed by a Hessian soldier. Her maiden name was Jane Holman, and she had three children, Samuel, William and Polly. After his return from the army he married a second wife, whose maiden name was Jane Sunderland, by whom he had ten children, five boys, Daniel, Henry, Peter, John and Frank; and five daughters, Elizabeth, Kathern, Nancy, Keziah and Jane.

Of the sons: Henry married Jennie Shaw and had three sons and five daughters; Daniel married Polly Clinton and had eight children; John married Polly Burns and had four children; Peter married Hannah Kennedy and had twelve children; Frank married Prudie Bell, no children.

Of the daughters: Jane married John Stoakes, Sr., and had eleven children; Keziah married William Stoakes, Jr., and had nine children; Nancy married John Cooper; Sarah married Alexander Cooper; Hetty married William Spitler.

Of the children who were bereft by the cruel act of the Hessian soldier we have no record, but presume they remained in New Jersey, as they were grown men and women when their father moved with his second family to Ohio, about twenty years after the close of the war. Later we learned that Samuel, the oldest, moved several years later to Ohio, and settled in Madison county. Their father, Henry, Sr., the Revolutionary soldier, rode on horse-back from New Jersey to eastern Ohio and bought land in Jefferson county, near Port Homer, which was a government fort, and in the autumn of 1801 brought his family from New Jersey. It was so late that he could not get his cabin completed before winter, and they were obliged to spend the winter in the fort, where his youngest daughter, Jane, was born in the early spring of 1802.

Of the three brothers who served in the army, John died young, William settled in Madison County, Ohio, and Henry in Jefferson County, Ohio. They lost their property in New Jersey by the failure of the government to redeem currency issued during the war, and consequently had limited means to start new homes on the frontier, but they were industrious and frugal and soon acquired a competence. The sons of Henry, Sr., when grown to manhood, settled, Daniel, Henry and Peter in or near Ashland, Ohio, and John and Frank near Mansfield, Ohio.

Later: Several descendants of the family who remained in New Jersey came to Ohio in the '40s, and settled near Akron, but we have no further record of them. Peter Vantilburg, a son of Henry, Sr., settled at Ashland, Ohio, and raised a family of twelve children. We only have a record of one of them, Vincent Vantilburg, and one of his sons, John M. Vantilburg, who now lives at Mansfield, Ohio. John Vantilburg, who settled at Mansfield, had three children. One of them, Daniel Vantilburg, went to Iowa in the late '60s, and bought a piece of land in Blackhawk county, on which he built a house and made improvements, but a few years later was caught in a blizzard on his way home from Waterloo and had to abandon his team and take refuge in a haystack, where he remained twenty-four hours, until the storm abated, and he succeeded in getting to the nearest house. His feet were so badly frozen that amputation was necessary, and he was left a cripple for life. He sold his farm and went back to Ohio, where he died a few years later. Another son of Henry Vantilburg, Sr., located at Ashland, Ohio, and raised a family there. One of his sons, Francis Vantilburg, raised a family of four children, all living in Ashland. They are: Herman D. Vantilburg, Mrs. Ida Vantilburg Nasters, Mrs. Jennie Vantilburg Wharton and Mrs. Lezzette Vantilburg Mason. Samuel Vantilburg, Sr., who settled in Madison County, Ohio, raised a large family and had many descendants. A complete genealogy of the Vantilburg family would require more time, correspondence and research than the author is able to devote to it in his present state of health and advanced age, and he will be obliged to leave a more complete work to younger hands.

RECORD OF THE FOUNDERS OF THE STOAKES FAMILY IN AMERICA.

Names	Date of Birth	Date of Marriage	Resident or Death
William Stoakes, Sr.	Not known	1789	Died Nov. 18, 1831
Ann Hall Stoakes	Not known	1789	Died March 7, 1831

Children of William Stoakes, Sr., and Ann (Hall) Stoakes.

Names	Date of Birth	Date of Marriage	Residence or Death
William Stoakes, Jr.	1789	Nov. 23, 1813	Died July 15, 1859
John Stoakes, Sr.	Aug. 1, 1792	Nov. 3, 1818	Died Feb. 11, 1879

Children of John Stoakes, Sr., and Jane (Vantilburg) Stoakes.

Names	Date of Birth	Date of Marriage	Residence or Death
Nancy Ann Stoakes	Aug. 6, 1819	July 28, 1842	Died April 3, 1894
Martha Jane Stoakes	March 15, 1821	Jan. 14, 1841	Died Jan. 9, 1910
William M. Stoakes	Dec. 26, 1823	May 27, 1847	Died Jan. 15, 1904
Henry C. Stoakes	May 3, 1825	Jan. 3, 1860	Died March 2, 1914
John R. Stoakes	Aug. 26, 1827	Dec. 23, 1851	Died Feb. 16, 1921
Elizabeth Stoakes	Aug. 16, 1830	March 11, 1851	Died Feb. 18, 1918
Eleazer Stoakes	March 4, 1833	March 1, 1866	Died Nov. 26, 1911
Katherine Stoakes	Nov. 10, 1836	Unmarried	Died April 12, 1841
Sarah E. Stoakes	March 17, 1838	Dec. 23, 1864	Died March 28, 1916
California Stoakes	Aug. 17, 1841	Unmarried	Died Feb. 3, 1919
George W. Stoakes	Sept. 14, 1843	Jan. 11, 1866	Traer, Iowa

RECORD OF THE NANCY ANN (STOAKES) AND JOHN RIDER FAMILY.

Nancy Ann (Stoakes) Rider, eldest daughter of John Stoakes, Sr., and Jane (Vantilburg) Stoakes, was born in Jefferson County, Ohio, and grew to womanhood there. In 1842 she married John Rider, and they resided in Wellsville, Ohio. About 1849 they moved to Wisconsin, where they lived a few years, and in 1852, during the "gold craze", went overland to California, where they located at Sacramento, and lived there the balance of their lives. From their settlement in Sacramento the Riders have taken an active part in public affairs, and have many descendants in California. One family, that of Edward Rider, had five out of six sons in the "World War". Mr. Rider died in 1902 and Mrs. Rider in 1894.

Children of John and Nancy Ann (Stoakes) Rider.

Names	Date of Birth	Date of Marriage	Residence or Death
George K. Rider	Oct. 14, 1844	March 28, 1881	Sacramento, Cal.
Martha Jane Rider	June 10, 1847	Unmarried	Died June 8, 1852
Catherine E. Rider	Nov. 4, 1848	Unmarried	Died Aug. 10, 1849
Henry Rider	Aug. 10, 1850	Unmarried	Died May 27, 1882
Frank Rider	Feb. 17, 1852	Unmarried	Died Aug. 21, 1898
William Rider	April 23, 1854	June 17, 1880	Died Apr. 15, 1920
Charles Rider	Aug. 19, 1855	June 17, 1903	Died Apr. 5, 1905
Edward Rider	Dec. 7, 1859	————, 1884	San Jose, Cal.

Husbands and Wives of Children of John and Nancy Ann (Stoakes) Rider.

George K. Rider, born in 1844, married March 28, 1881. Wife, Anna Egan. No children. Residence, Sacramento, Cal.

William Rider, born April 23, 1854, married June 17, 1880; died April 5, 1920. Wife, Ann E. Qeale.

Charles Rider, born Aug. 19, 1855, married June 1903, died April 5, 1905. Wife, Flora V. Stoakes, born March 31, 1855. No children. Residence, San Leandro, Cal.

Edward Rider, born Dec. 7, 1859, married 1884. Wife, Agnes Harkness, born 1860. Residence, San Jose, Cal.

Children of William and Ann (Qeale) Rider

Genevieve Rider, born Feb. 10, 1883, married Jan. 15, 1903. Husband, Lew A. Wallace. Son, Lew Wallace, Jr., born March 21, 1904. Residence, Fair Oaks, Cal.

William Rider, Jr., born May 24, 1902. Residence, Fair Oaks, Cal.

Children of Edward and Agnes (Harkness) Rider

Frederick C. Rider, born 1884; unmarried; residence, San Jose, Cal.

Hazel E. Rider, born Aug. 19, 1885; married Oct. 8, 1906; residence, Sacramento, Cal.

Fergus Rider, born 1887; unmarried; residence, San Jose, Cal.

Harry Rider, born 1889; unmarried; residence, San Jose, Cal.

Azalia Rider, born Oct. 7, 1892; unmarried; residence, San Jose, Cal.

John Rider, Jr., born 1894; married 1916; residence, Lakeport, Cal.

Edward Rider, Jr., born 1896; unmarried; residence, San Jose, Cal.

Bessie Rider, born Oct. 9, 1897; unmarried; residence, San Jose, Cal.

George Rider, Jr., born 1900; unmarried; residence, San Jose, Cal.

Children of John Rider, Jr., and Dorothy (Bacchus) Rider

Agnes Elizabeth Rider, born 1918. Dorothy Margaret Rider, born Nov. 4, 1920. Residence, Lakeport, Cal.

Note:—Of the six sons of Edward and Agnes (Harkness) Rider, five served in the "World War".

RECORD OF THE HOPKINS BRANCH OF THE JOHN STOAKES, SR. FAMILY.

Martha Jane (Stoakes) Hopkins, second daughter of John Stoakes, Sr., was born in 1821, and grew to womanhood in the family home. In 1841 she married J. P Hopkins, who came to that locality from Portage County, Ohio. They lived on the Stoakes farm until the fall of 1847, when they moved to Wellsville, in Columbiana County. Their only children were John S., the writer of this history, who was born in 1842, and Nancy Ellen, born in 1847, who died in infancy. After moving to Wellsville, Ohio, in the fall of 1847, Mr. Hopkins engaged in business with his father-in-law, John Stoakes, Sr., and his brother-in-law, Henry C. Stoakes, as partners. His health failed him and he died in 1849. In 1851 Mrs. Hopkins married L. S. Cope, a widower with one daughter, a young lady, who died in 1852. In 1854 Mr. Cope, wife and the writer came to Iowa, and in 1855 settled on a prairie farm in Tama County. They lived on the farm until 1866, when they moved to Waterloo, Iowa, where Mrs. Cope started a millinery store, in which business she continued until 1882. Mr. Cope died in 1873, leaving her a second time a widow. In the fall of 1878 she moved her millinery business to Traer, where she continued that business until 1882, when she married John Wilson, Sr., and they went to his farm four miles west of Traer, on which they remained a few years and then returned to Traer. Mr. Wilson died in the spring of 1892, leaving Mrs. Wilson for the third time a widow. She survived Mr. Wilson nearly 18 years, dying January 3, 1910, at the ripe old age of near 89 years. She was buried beside Mr. Wilson in the Buckingham cemetery. Her only living child, the writer, is the head of a large family, and has resided for the past thirty-seven years in Humboldt County, Iowa.

The Hopkins-Stoakes Branch of the John Stoakes, Sr., Family

Names	Date of Birth	Date of Marriage	Residence or Death
Martha Jane Stoakes	March 15, 1821	January 14, 1841	Died Jan. 8, 1910
Josiah P. Hopkins	April 29, 1814	January 14, 1841	Died July 9, 1849

Children of Josiah P. and Martha Jane (Stoakes) Hopkins

Names	Date of Birth	Date of Marriage	Residence or Death
John S. Hopkins	March 1, 1842	May 19, 1864	Bradgate, Iowa
Nancy Ellen Hopkins	March 11, 1847	Unmarried	Died Aug. 9, 1848

Children of John S. and Mary F. (Messer) Hopkins

Frank Fremont Hopkins, born Nov. 13, 1865; married May, 1893. First wife, Margaret Anderson, died July 12, 1904. Second wife, Winnifred Comstock, married 1907. Residence, Chicago, Ill.

Mary C. Hopkins, born Nov. 9, 1868; married 1887. Residence Spencer, Iowa Husband, William Lancaster, born 1860; died Feb. 18, 1921.

Martha C. Hopkins, born Feb. 13, 1872; married 1892. Husband, William C. Hoag, born 1872. Residence, Ottosen, Iowa, R. F. D. 2.

Nellie E. Hopkins, born June 3, 1874; married Oct. 17, 1894. Husband, Downer White. Residence, Vinita, Okla.

Samuel T. Hopkins, born Dec. 6, 1876; married Dec. 6, 1900. First wife, Nellie Whitmore, died Dec. 5, 1903. Second wife, Emma Williams, married Sept. 6, 1905. Residence, Vancouver, Washington.

Maude S. Hopkins, born April 2, 1880; married Jan. 7, 1904. Husband, Victor H. Vilmont. Residence, Eldora, Iowa.

Wilson P. Hopkins, born July 17, 1883. Unmarried. Residence Chicago, Ill.

Lucinda Hopkins, born Oct. 10, 1887; married July 1, 1908. Husband, C. C. Knoll. Residence, Gilmore City, Iowa.

Clifford G. Hopkins, born Jan. 4, 1891; married 1910. Wife, Elizabeth Shultz, born Nov. 5, 1892. Residence, Chicago, Ill.

Grand Children of John S. and Mary F. (Messer) Hopkins

Daughter of Frank and Winnifred (Comstock) Hopkins

Margaret Hopkins, born May, 1908. Residence, Chicago, Ill.

Children of William and Mary C. (Hopkins) Lancaster

Irene Lancaster, born June 23, 1888; married June 23, 1908. Husband, William Nielson. Daughter, Winnifred Nielsen, born 1909. Residence, Los Angeles, Cal.

Amy Lancaster, born May 26, 1890. Unmarried. Residence,
Spencer, Iowa.

Dora Lancaster, born Nov. 9, 1891; died June 22, 1913. Unmarried.

Kenneth Lancaster, born Sept. 11, 1897. Unmarried. Residence,
Spencer, Iowa.

Children of William C. and Martha (Hopkins) Hoag

Lenore R. Hoag, born July 15, 1893. Husband, Leroy Adams. Married 1916. Son, Leroy Linn Adams, born March 21, 1917. Son, Gorman Hoag Adams, born April 20, 1921. Residence, Bradgate, Iowa, R. F. D. 1.

Mildred E. Hoag, born July 15, 1895. Died Jan. 30, 1915. Unmarried.

Marian E. Hoag, born Aug. 24, 1896. Husband, Theron E. Kendall. Married 1916. Children, Therese Mildred Kendall, born Sept. 22, 1917; Virgil Theron Kendall, born Oct. 1, 1919. Residence Ottosen, Iowa, R. F. D. 2.

Conlee S. Hoag, born April 2, 1898. Married 1919. Wife, Ethel M. Saddler. Son, William Conlee Hoag, born March 15, 1921. Residence, Ottosen, Iowa, R. F. D. 2.

Rollin E. Hoag, born March 19, 1900. Married May 7, 1921. Wife, Helen J. Mather. Residence, Bradgate, Iowa.

Gertrude M. Hoag, born April 20, 1902.

Edna G. Hoag, born July 24, 1904.

Dorris G. Hoag, born April 10, 1907.

Gretta H. Hoag, born May 18, 1910.

Beulah N. Hoag, born June 24, 1912.

Baby Charlotte Hoag, born Jan. 14, 1916. Died Dec. 31, 1916.

Family home, Ottosen, Iowa, R. F. D. 2.

Children of Downer and Nellie E. (Hopkins) White

Rhoda White, born Jan. 23, 1896. Married Oct. 17, 1917. Husband, Robert H. Martine. Residence, Greene, Kansas.

Paul White, born Sept. 28, 1899. Residence, Vinita, Okla.

Raymond White, born Aug. 20, 1905. Died, Aug. 27, 1905.

Carroll White, born Aug. 8, 1909. Residence, Vinita, Okla.

Son of Samuel T. and Nellie (Whitmore) Hopkins

Louis L. Hopkins, born Dec. 7, 1901. In U. S. Service, Manilla, P. I.

Son of Samuel T. and Emma (Williams) Hopkins

Stanley W. Hopkins, born Nov. 30, 1910. Residence, Vancouver, Wash.

Children of Victor and Maude (Hopkins) Vilmont

Maurice Vilmont, born August 7, 1907, Eldora, Iowa.

Bernice Vilmont, born November 17, 1908. Eldora, Iowa.

Marjorie Vilmont, born March 11, 1910. Eldora, Iowa.

Children of C. C. and Lucinda (Hopkins) Knoll

Stanley M. Knoll, born April 18, 1912. Gilmore City, Iowa.

Sterling H. Knoll, born January 20, 1914. Gilmore City, Iowa.

Children of Clifford G. and Elizabeth (Shultz) Hopkins

Leonard Hopkins, born March 1, 1911. Chicago, Ill.

Raymond Hopkins, born August 20, 1912. Chicago, Ill.

Clifford Hopkins, Jr., born October 3, 1914. Chicago, Ill.

Beverly Hopkins, born August 14, 1916. Chicago, Ill.

Beatrice Hopkins, born August 31, 1918. Chicago, Ill.

RECORD OF THE WILLIAM M. AND CAROLINE (HOUSE-HOLDER) STOAKES FAMILY.

William M. Stokes, oldest son of John Stoakes, Sr., and Jane (Vantilburg) Stoakes, was born in Jefferson County, Ohio, in 1823. He grew to manhood on the mill farm of his father, and on attaining his majority, farmed a few years with J. P. Hopkins on the south part of the farm. In 1847, at the age of twenty-four, he married Caroline Householder, daughter of Matthias and Susan Householder, who were early settlers in Jefferson County. After marriage he continued to work his father's main farm until 1851, when he moved to Van Buren County, Iowa. On leaving here he moved in February, 1855, to Tama County, Iowa, where he had purchased a prairie farm and built a cabin in the fall of 1854. He improved and added to this until he owned a large farm of as good land as could be found in Iowa. He raised a family of twelve children, most of whom remained in the neighborhood of the parental home. He died in 1904, at the age of eighty-one years. Mrs. Stoakes survived him ten years, dying in 1914.

William M. and Caroline (Householder) Stoakes

Names	Date of Birth	Date of Marriage	Residence or Death
William M. Stoakes	Dec. 23, 1823	May 27, 1847	Died Jan. 15, 1904
Caroline Stoakes	July 10, 1829	May 27, 1847	Died June 14, 1914

Children of William M. and Caroline (Householder) Stoakes

Matthias Stoakes, born Jan. 18, 1848; married Oct. 27, 1874. Wife, Jane Stewart, born Dec. 28, 1846. Residence, Traer, Iowa.

John N. Stoakes, born Aug. 7, 1849; died May 14, 1910. Wife, Mary Brown, born Feb. 23, 1846; died Nov. 4, 1917.

Ann Eliza Stoakes, born Nov. 21, 1851; died June 5, 1861.

William H. Stoakes, born 1853; married 1876. Wife, Alice Jameyson. Residence, Albion, Neb.

Frank Stoakes, born April 29, 1855; died Nov. 15, 1870.

Jane Stoakes, born April 17, 1858; married Dec. 9, 1880; died Nov. 17, 1918. Husband, William McAlevy, died Sept. 2, 1910.

Charles Stoakes, born April 21, 1859; died Nov. 3, 1876.

Arabella Stoakes, born Oct. 8, 1862; unmarried. Residence, Traer, Iowa.

Walter C. Stoakes, born May 25, 1864; married Aug. 19, 1890. Wife, Phoebe Parks, born July 30, 1863. Residence, Traer, Iowa.

Mason J. Stoakes, born Feb. 25, 1866; married Feb. 15, 1899. Wife, Minnie McDowell, born Jan. 20, 1873. Residence, Traer, Iowa.

Carrie Stoakes, born 1867; married 1890. Husband, John L. Thomas, born 1865. Residence, Traer, Iowa.

Bennett R. Stoakes, born Aug. 29, 1868; unmarried. Residence, Traer, Iowa.

Edward Stoakes, born Sept. 23, 1870; married Dec. 14, 1898. Wife, Agnes Logan, born March 12, 1871. Residence, Traer, Iowa.

GRANDCHILDREN AND GREAT-GRANDCHILDREN OF WILLIAM M. AND CAROLINE STOAKES.

RECORD OF MATTHIAS AND JANE (STEWART) STOAKES FAMILY

Matthias Stoakes, oldest son of William and Caroline Stoakes was born in Jefferson County, Ohio, January 14, 1848, and moved to Tama County, Iowa, when a boy, in 1855. When grown to manhood he bought a farm and his since lived on it continuously. In 1874 he married Jane Stewart, a school teacher from Wisconsin. They raised a family of six children, all of whom are now living. Their farm of 240 acres is highly improved, and located five miles east of the town of Traer. Mr. Stoakes and his younger son, Frank, Jr., are engaged in farming and fine stock raising.

Children of Matthias and Jane (Stewart) Stoakes

Ella Stoakes, born Nov. 1, 1875; unmarried. Residence, Traer, Ia.

Charles Stoakes, born Aug. 22, 1877; married Dec. 23, 1911. Wife, Margaret H. Wolfman, born Aug. 18, 1882. Residence, Battle Creek, Iowa.

William Matthias Stoakes, born June 24, 1879; unmarried. Residence, Terrill, Iowa.

Edith Elizabeth Stoakes, born June 14, 1881; married Nov. 18, 1903. Husband, John Wilson Flemming, born Oct. 6, 1873. Residence, Grundy Center, Iowa.

John Roy Stoakes, born Sept. 11, 1883; married Dec. 25, 1911. Wife, Catherine Voght, born Oct. 3, 1878. Residence, Traer, Iowa.

Frank Ray Stoakes, born Nov. 23, 1884; unmarried. Residence, Traer, Iowa.

Grandchildren of Matthias and Jane (Stewart) Stoakes

Children of Charles and Margaret (Wolfman) Stoakes

Anna Jane Stoakes, born Dec. 24, 1912.
James Stewart Stoakes, born March 8, 1915.
Charles Franklin Stoakes, born July 15, 1918.
Residence, Battle Creek, Iowa.

Children of Edith Elizabeth (Stoakes) and John W. Flemming

Ray Stewart Flemming, born Nov. 16, 1904.
Grace Elizabeth Flemming, born July 17, 1906.
Ruth Matilda Flemming, born Jan. 23, 1908.
Vera Lucille Flemming, born Nov. 28, 1912.
Residence, Grundy Center, Iowa.

Children of John Roy and Catherine (Voght) Stoakes

Russell Mathias Stoakes, born June 22, 1911.
John Raymond Stoakes, born June 23, 1913.
Residence, Traer, Iowa.

RECORD OF THE JOHN N. AND MARY (BROWN) STOAKES FAMILY.

John N. Stoakes, second son of William M. and Caroline H. Stoakes, was born in Jefferson County, Ohio, Aug. 7, 1849, and came west with his parents in 1851. He grew to manhood in Tama County, Iowa, and engaged in farming. About 1870 he married Mary Brown, and continued to live on the farm for many years, but finally sold his farm and moved to Traer, where he engaged in the machinery and farm implement business. He later went into the musical instrument business, and continued in that line until his death in 1910. His wife died in 1917. They raised a family of five children.

Children of John N. and Mary (Brown) Stoakes

Thomas F. Stoakes, born May 27, 1872; married. Wife, Elizabeth Huey Calderwood. Residence, Traer, Iowa.

Maggie B. Stoakes, born June 28, 1874; married. Husband, John Pippert. Residence, Dysart, Iowa.

Ernest R. Stoakes, born Nov. 1, 1876; married June 28, 1899. Wife, Fannie Fern, born March 17, 1873. Residence, Maple Hill, Iowa.

Anna C. Stoakes, born April 5, 1880; married. Husband, George B. Vandenburg. Residence, Armstrong, Iowa.

Grace G. Stoakes, born August 14, 1882; married. Husband, Rasmus Watne. Residence, Eagle Grove, Iowa.

Grandchildren of John N. and Mary (Brown) Stoakes

Children of John and Maggie B. (Stoakes) Pippert

Bruce Pippert, born Feb. 10, 1902.

Seward S. Pippert, born April 2, 1906. Died March 24, 1911.

Miriam Pippert, born Jan. 29, 1908.

Richard S. Pippert, born July 8, 1910.

Bernice Pippert, born April 10, 1912.

Residence, Dysart, Iowa.

Children of Ernest and Fannie (Fern) Stoakes

Gladys Stoakes, born April 23, 1900; died April 23, 1900.

Kenneth S. Stoakes, born Dec. 17, 1901.

Duayne W. Stoakes, born Feb. 17, 1903.

Jessie Gerald Stoakes, born March 16, 1904.

Frederick Fern Stoakes, born Aug. 27, 1907.

John Norman Stoakes, born Sept. 14, 1911.

Herbert Donald Stoakes, born June 6, 1913.

Residence, Maple Hill, Iowa.

Children of George B. and Anna C. (Stoakes) Vandenburg

Leroy U. Vandenburg, born Sept. 11, 1907.

Edward S. Vandenburg, born May 10, 1912.

Margaret Vandenburg, born March 3, 1916.

Residence, Armstrong, Iowa.

RECORD OF THE WILLIAM H. AND ALICE (JAMEYSON) STOAKES FAMILY.

Dr. William H. Stoakes was born in 1853, in Van Buren County, Iowa, and went with his parents in 1855 to Tama County, Iowa, where he grew to manhood. In 1876 he was married to Alice Jameyson, and they commenced housekeeping on a farm east of Traer, Iowa. Owing to a physical disability he decided to leave the farm and study for the medical profession. He went to the Iowa State University and graduated from the Homeopathic department. He commenced practice in Bradgate, Humboldt County, Iowa, but later moved to Humboldt, and finally to Albion, Neb., where he is now located and has built up a fine practice. Dr. and Mrs. Stoakes have raised a family of eight children, all living, and six of them married and have families and homes.

Children of William H. and Alice (Jameyson) Stoakes

Irene E. Stoakes, born Nov. 29, 1877; married. Husband, W. C. Maxwell. Residence, Albion, Neb.

C. Ralph Stoakes, born Jan. 24, 1880; married. Wife, Rose Elliott. Residence, Fort Dodge, Iowa.

Wm. Howard Stoakes, born Feb. 20, 1883; married April 22, 1906. Wife, Bessie Brown, born April 29, 1882. Residence, Humboldt, Iowa.

Roger Stoakes, born Sept. 24, 1884; married. Wife, Mable Cook. Residence, Albion, Neb.

Hazel M. Stoakes, born March 9, 1887; married. Husband, J. V. Cook. Residence, Norfolk, Neb.

Lee C. Stoakes, born July 16, 1889; unmarried. Residence, Jewell, Iowa.

Ruby A. Stoakes, born Aug. 9, 1893; married. Husband, Roy Williamson. Residence, Albion, Neb.

Naomi Stoakes, born March 10, 1901; unmarried. Residence, Albion, Neb.

Grandchildren of William H. and Alice J. Stoakes

Children of W. C. and Irene (Stoakes) Maxwell

Carroll M. and Champe S. Maxwell. Residence, Albion, Neb.

Children of C. Ralph and Rose (Elliott) Stoakes

Madine S. Stoakes.

Harold S. Stoakes.

Virginia Gertrude, Gilbert Cope, and William Levi Stoakes, triplets, born May 19th, 1921, at Fort Dodge, Iowa.

(Note: So far as is recorded this is the first birth of triplets in the history of the Stoakes family. This announcement was received just in time to be included in the family history.)

Residence, Fort Dodge, Iowa.

Children of Wm. Howard and Bessie (Brown) Stoakes

Marie Hazel Stoakes, born July 19, 1907.

Elmer Howard Stoakes, born April 29, 1910.

Marjorie Alice Stoakes, born August 23, 1912.

Residence,   Humboldt, Iowa

Children of Roger and Mable (Cook) Stoakes.

Lester, Gordon, Mason and Mina Stoakes.   Residence, Albion, Neb.

Children of J. V. and Hazel M. (Stoakes) Cook

William, Levern and Robert B. Cook.   Residence, Norfolk, Neb.
Virginia Cook, born Oct. 30, 1916; died Oct. 20, 1918.

Child of Roy and Ruby A. (Stoakes) Williamson

Margaret Williamson.   Residence, Albion, Neb.

RECORD OF THE WILLIAM AND JANE (STOAKES) McALEVY FAMILY

Jane Stoakes, born April 17, 1858; married Dec. 9, 1880. Died Nov. 17, 1918. Husband, William McAlevy. Died Sept. 2 1910.

Children of William and Jane (Stoakes) McAlevy

Edward McAlevy, born April 1, 1888; married July 15, 1912. Wife Anna Finseth. Residence, Sioux City, Iowa.

Paul McAlevy, born May 21, 1892; married June 15, 1917. Wife Emma J. Anderson. No children. Residence, Omaha, Neb

Children of Edward and Anna (Finseth) McAlevy

Ronald E. McAlevy, born April 27, 1913.

Maxine McAlevy, born April 24, 1918.

Residence, Sioux City, Iowa.

RECORD OF THE WALTER C. AND PHOEBE (PARKS) STOAKES FAMILY.

Walter C. Stoakes, born May 25, 1864; married August 19, 1890. Wife, Phoebe Parks, born July 30, 1862. Residence, Traer, Iowa.

Children of Walter C. and Phoebe (Parks) Stoakes

Beulah Stoakes, born Jan. 3, 1892; married Feb. 9, 1916. Died March 21, 1920. Husband, Peter Wilson. Residence, Traer, Iowa.

RECORD OF THE MASON J. AND MINNIE (McDOWALL) STOAKES FAMILY.

Mason J. Staokes, born Feb. 25, 1866; married Feb. 15, 1899. Wife, Minnie McDowall, born Jan. 20, 1873. Residence, Traer, Iowa.

Daughter of Mason J. and Minnie (McDowall) Stoakes

Elizabeth Stoakes, born April, 1909. Traer, Iowa.

RECORD OF THE JOHN L. AND CARRIE (STOAKES) THOMAS FAMILY.

Carrie Stoakes, born 1867; married 1890. Husband, John L. Thomas, born 1865. Residence, Traer, Iowa.

Children of John L. and Carrie (Stoakes) Thomas

Ruth Thomas, born 1891. Unmarried. Residence, Traer, Iowa.
Paul Thomas, born 1894. Married. Wife, Zenaide Kahler. Residence, Traer, Iowa.

Children of Paul and Zenaide (Kahler) Thomas

Virginia Thomas, born 1916.
John Robert Thomas, born 1918.

Residence, Traer, Iowa.

RECORD OF THE EDWARD AND AGNES (LOGAN) STOAKES FAMILY.

Edward Stoakes, born Sept. 28, 1870; married Dec. 14, 1898. Wife Agnes Logan, born March 12, 1871. Residence, Traer, Iowa.

Children of Edward and Agnes (Logan) Stoakes

Jeannette Stoakes, born Nov. 13, 1905.
Paul Stoakes, born Jan. 1907.

Residence, Traer, Iowa.

RECORD OF THE HENRY C. AND ARMILDA (HOUGH) STOAKES FAMILY.

Henry C. Stoakes, second son of John Stoakes, Sr., and Jane (Vantilburg) Stoakes, was born on the home farm in 1825, and grew to manhood there. In 1848 he moved to Wellsville, Ohio, and went into partnership with his father and J. P. Hopkins, in the wholesale grocery business. In 1854 he moved with the unmarried members of his father's family, to Van Buren County, Iowa. In 1854 he purchased land in Tama County, Iowa, and farmed for many years. In 1860 he was married to Armilda Hough, daughter of Robert and Julia Hough, who came from Indiana. Henry and wife raised a large family, most of them born

in Tama County. About 1880 he sold the Tama County farm
and moved to O'Brien County, Iowa. Here he farmed for a few
years and next moved to Western Nebraska. Here he remained
a few years and next went to Southern Missouri, near the town
of Bolivar, where he resided the remainder of his life. He died
in 1914, aged eighty-nine years. Mrs. Stoakes died in 1913. Most
of their large family live in Southwest Missouri, and adjoining
states.

**Children and Grand-Children of Henry C. and Armilda (Hough)
Stoakes.**

Cora Stoakes, born Oct. 24, 1860; married. Husband, Jesse Morse.
Residence, Delaware, Okla.

John R. Stoakes, Jr. (2) born May 18, 1862; unmarried. Residence, Minnesota.

Marion F. Stoakes, born May 4, 1863; unmarried; died May 14,
1895.

Robert E. Stoakes, born Dec. 24, 1864; married. Residence, Bolivar, Missouri.

Henry Sherman Stoakes, born Nov. 27, 1866; married Feb. 1893.
Wife, Minnie Stoakes. Residence, Bolivar, Mo.
Daughters, Hazel Lucile and Mary Inez; son, Carew.
Mary Inez Stoakes, married. Husband, Anthony Sholtz, residence, Portland, Ore. Son, Robert Sherman Sholtz, born 1916.

May Belle Stoakes, born Oct. 14, 1868; married Oct. 14, 1898.
Husband, Frank Lovell. Residence, North Platte, Neb. Children: Clifford M. Lovell, born Aug. 16, 1901, died Oct. 16,
1901. Harry Edward Lovell, born Dec. 17, 1902; married
Feb. 23, 1918. Wife, Ila M. Parks. Residence, North Platte,
Neb.

Mary Inez Stoakes, born March 3, 1870; married March, 1888.
Husband, F. Dentler. Residence, New York City. Children:
Marion Dentler, born Feb. 28, 1891.

Helen Azalia Dentler, born March 17, 1889, married, husband, Harry Lord; daughter, Ruth Lord, born May 1918. Residence,
New York City.

Harry Stoakes, born Nov. 15, 1875; unmarried. Residence, Bolivar, Mo.

Ralph Stoakes, born Dec. 8, 1878; married Dec. 1919. Residence,
Joplin, Mo.

Roy Stoakes, born Dec. 6, 1879; married Dec. 30, 1905.   Wife,
Myrtle Wells. Residence, Bolivar, Mo. Children: Glenn
Stoakes, born Dec. 1, 1906; Fern Stoakes, born Dec. 31, 1908.
Residence, Bolivar, Mo.

Benjamin Franklin Stoakes, (2) born Nov. 17, 1880; unmarried.
Residence, Bolivar, Mo.

Julia Etta Stoakes, born Nov. 17, 1886; married. Husband, Lee
Fisher. Residence, Joplin, Mo.

RECORD OF THE JOHN R. AND ELIZABETH (STEVENSON) STOAKES FAMILY.

John R. Stoakes, third son of John Stoakes, Sr., was born on
the Yellow Creek farm in Jefferson County, in 1827, and lived
there until the family moved in 1843, to Wellsville, Columbiana
County, Ohio, where he entered the employ of the Cleveland-Pitts-
burg Railroad company, the terminus of which was then at Wellsville. He continued in the service of the company almost fifty
years, when at the age of seventy years, he was retired on a pen-
sion for life. In 1851 he married Elizabeth Stevenson. They
were the parents of six children, two of whom, Henry and Mary
J. are still living in Wellsville. Henry is a machinist and lived
with his father and sister, Mary, having lost his wife several
years ago. He had no children. Mary J., the youngest of the
John R. Stoakes family, is not married and has made her home
with her father and brother, Henry. She has been a teacher for
many years and is now principal of the East Wellsville schools.
The rest of the children have passed away. Mrs. Stoakes died in
1903, and Mr. Stoakes died Feb. 18, 1921, at the age of ninety-
three years. He was the oldest of all the Stoakes family, living
or dead.

John R. and Elizabeth (Stevenson) Stoakes

Name	Date of Birth	Date of Marriage	Residence or Death
John R. Stoakes	Aug 26, 1827	Dec. 23, 1851	Feb. 18, 1921
Elizabeth Stevenson	————————	Dec. 23, 1851	July 27, 1903

Children of John R. and Elizabeth S. Stoakes

James Henry Stoakes, born Sept. 23, 1852; married. Residence,
Wellsville, Ohio. Wife, Oella Bright, died Oct. 13, 1909.

John G. Stoakes, born Aug. 22, 1854; married. Died May 15, 1910.
Wife, Elizabeth Blue, residence. Wellsville, Ohio.

George P. Stoakes, born June 1, 1856; died Aug. 21, 1862.

Thomas B. Stoakes, born Dec. 28, 1857; married. Died Feb. 28, 1915. Wife, Jennie M. Prosser, residence, Wellsville, Ohio.

Mary Jane Stoakes, born July 31, 1862; unmarried. Residence, Wellsville, Ohio.

Grand-Children of John R. and Elizabeth S. Stoakes

Children of John G. and Elizabeth (Blue) Stoakes

Wilson Stoakes, born April 6, 1883; died April 25, 1900.

Edward B. Stoakes, born March, 1885; died Nov. 3, 1885.

Lawrence Mitchell Stoakes, born Oct. 3, 1886. Residence, Pittsburg, Pa.

Harry M. Stoakes, born July 25, 1890. Died ————

Robert S. Stoakes, born Oct. 3, 1893; unmarried. Residence, Pittsburg, Pa.

John P. Stoakes, born July 11, 1897; unmarried. Residence, Pittsburg, Pa.

Children of Thomas B. and Jennie (Prosser) Stoakes

Grace L. Stoakes, born March 29, 1882. Residence, Cleveland, Ohio.

William C. Stoakes, born Nov. 23, 1886; married Oct. 17, 1919. Wife, Margaret Scott. Residence, Cleveland, Ohio.

Irene B. Stoakes, born Nov. 27, 1889; married 1909. Husband, Ramond Brisbane. Children: Dorothy Jane Brisbane, born Oct. 16, 1910. Richard Brisbane, born 1914. Residence, Pittsburg, Pa.

RECORD OF THE GASTON BRANCH OF THE JOHN STOAKES, SR. FAMILY

Elizabeth (Stoakes) Gaston was born in 1830 at the family home in Jefferson County, Ohio, and grew to womanhood there. In 1851 at the parental home in Wellsville, Ohio, she was married to Hugh Gaston, a merchant of Knoxville, Ohio. In 1854, Mr. Gaston, wife and daughter, Marietta, moved to Iowa, settling in the fall of that year on a farm which he bought in Perry township, Tama County, Iowa, one mile northeast of the present town of

Traer. Here they raised quite a large family and remained on the farm for over fifty years. They then built a residence in Traer and rented the farm to two of their sons. Later they sold the farm and remained in Traer until they died, Mr. Gaston in 1916, at the age of ninety-five years, and Mrs. Gaston in 1918 at the age of eighty-eight.

Record of the Hugh and Elizabeth (Stoakes) Gaston Family

Names	Date of Birth	Date of Marriage	Residence or Death
Elizabeth Stoakes	Aug. 16, 1830	March 11, 1851	Died 1918
Hugh F. Gaston	Aug. 16, 1821	March 11, 1851	Died 1916

Children of Hugh F. and Elizabeth (Stoakes) Gaston

Marietta Gaston, born April 14, 1853; unmarried. Residence, Traer, Iowa.

James Gaston, born May 3, 1855; unmarried. Died Jan. 12, 1898.

Ella Gaston, born Dec. 30, 1856; married. Died March 28, 1898. Husband, Ovid P. Barbour.

John S. Gaston, born Jan. 3, 1859; married Nov. 22, 1888. Wife, Lena Schroeder. Residence, Boone, Iowa.

Mattie Gaston, born Dec. 11, 1860; unmarried. Died March 26, 1882.

W. W. Gaston, born May 28, 1863; married June 27, 1900. Wife, Anna Stewart. Residence, Waterloo, Iowa.

Azalia Gaston, born Sept. 16, 1865; married. First husband, ———Dyal, died———. Second husband, George Franzenburg. Residence, Tacoma, Wash.

Wallace D. Gaston, born March 23, 1868; married. Wife, Minnie Conrad. Residence, Traer, Iowa.

D. D. Gaston, born Oct. 11, 1870; unmarried. Residence, Traer, Iowa.

Grand Children of Hugh F. and Elizabeth (Stoakes) Gaston

Children of Ovid P. and Ella (Gaston) Barbour

Hugh Barbour, born Nov. 5, 1882; married. Wife, Inez Dodds. Residence, Wichita, Kansas.

Gretchen Barbour, born Feb. 22, 1890; married. Husband, Joseph N. Hamilton. Residence, Ponca City, Okla.

Hobart Barbour, born Feb. 22, 1891; married. Wife, Beulah Johnson. Residence, Wichita, Kansas.

Children of John S. and Lena (Schroeder) Gaston

Mildred Gaston, born Nov. 18, 1889; married Feb. 11, 1914. Husband, J. M. Gould. Children: Helen Elizabeth Gould, born June 22, 1917; Marcia Louisa Gould, born June 16, 1919. Residence, Boone, Iowa.

Mary Elizabeth Gaston, born Nov. 16, 1894; married Nov. 24, 1917. Husband, Dr. J. W. Duffy. Daughter, Mildred Jean Duffy, born Nov. 11, 1919. Residence, Chattanooga, Tenn.

Donald S. Gaston, born April 17, 1899; unmarried. Residence, Boone, Iowa.

Children of W. W. and Anna (Stewart) Gaston

Hazel Margaret Gaston, born July 30, 1903.
Dorris Elizabeth Gaston, born Oct. 4, 1904.
Marion Alberta Gaston, born March 18, 1907.
Esther Anna Gaston, born July 6, 1909.
Gretchen Evangeline Gaston, born March 16, 1912.

Residence, Waterloo, Iowa.

Children of Wallace and Minnie (Conrad) Gaston

Genevieve Gaston, born Dec. 2, 1901.
Russell Gaston, born Feb. 21, 1903.
Conrad Gaston, born Aug. 29, 1905.
Lyle Gaston, born July 29, 1909.

Residence, Traer, Iowa.

RECORD OF THE ELEAZER STOAKES BRANCH OF THE JOHN STOAKES, SR., FAMILY

Eleazer Stoakes, fourth son of John Stoakes, Sr., was born in 1833 on the home farm on Yellow Creek, and grew to manhood there. He came to Iowa and made his home with his father's family until the Civil War, when he enlisted in the 14th Iowa Volunteer Infantry. He was captured with his regiment at Pittsburg Landing, but was exchanged and soon after was discharged on account of sickness. After recovering, he bought a farm, and in 1866 married Eliza Granger, daughter of Robert and Mary Granger, who were early settlers in Northern Tama County. They

were the parents of six children, five of whom are still living, all
but one near the old home.   Mr. Stoakes died Nov. 26, 1911. Mrs.
Stoakes and two unmarried daughters live in Traer, Iowa.

Record of the Eleazer and Eliza (Granger) Stoakes Family

Names	Date of Birth	Date of Marriage	Residence or Death
Eleazer Stoakes	March 4, 1833	March 1, 1866	Died, Nov. 28, 1911
Eliza Granger	Dec. 11, 1842	March 1, 1866	Res., Traer, Iowa

Children of Eleazer and Eliza (Granger) Stoakes

Theodore G. Stoakes, born Jan. 28, 1867; married Jan. 18, 1893.
Wife, Sarah Kober, born Sept. 1, 1870. Residence, Traer, Iowa.

George E. Stoakes, born May 26, 1868; married July 27, 1899.
Wife, Minnie Vogt, born Jan. 23, 1876.   Residence, Traer,
Iowa.

Dewitt C. Stoakes, born June 22, 1870; died March 28, 1884.

Alice V. Stoakes, born Sept. 12, 1874; unmarried.   Residence,
Traer, Iowa.

Ella Mae Stoakes, born Aug. 30, 1877; unmarried.   Residence,
Traer, Iowa.

Mary Belle Stoakes, born March 7, 1881; married June 21, 1905.
Husband, Grant Pollock, born May 16, 1880. Residence, Rolfe,
Iowa.

Grand-Children of Eleazer and Eliza (Granger) Stoakes

Children of Theodore G. and Sarah (Kober) Stoakes

Newell Stoakes, born March 18, 1896; married March 31, 1918.
Wife, Julia Myers, born May 5, 1896. Residence, Traer, Ia.

Earl Stoakes, born March 23, 1898; married August 22, 1919.
Wife, Daisy Carter, born March 28, 1898. Residence, Traer
Iowa.

Children of George E. and Minnie (Vogt) Stoakes

Fred V. Stoakes, born August 27, 1901.
Florence Eliza Stoakes, born March 20, 1905.
Anna Mae Stoakes, born March 6, 1908.
Elsie Belle Stoakes, born Jan. 15, 1914.
George Robert Stoakes, born May 31, 1919.
Residence, Traer, Iowa.

Children of Grant and Mary Belle (Stoakes) Pollock

Cora Belle Pollock, born Oct. 11, 1906.
Robert Boyd Pollock, born July 20, 1908.
Margaret Eliza Pollock, born March 26, 1910.
Mary Mildred Pollock, born Aug. 22, 1913.
Jean Pollock, born Oct. 14, 1915. *Died Jan 27 1951*

Residence, Rolfe, Iowa.

THE THOMAS BRANCH OF THE JOHN STOAKES, SR., FAMILY

Sarah E. Stoakes, fourth daughter of John Stoakes, Sr., and Jane (Vantilburg) Stoakes, was born in Ohio in 1838 and came with the family to Iowa and settled with them in Tama County. In 1866 she was married to Benjamin Franklin Thomas, a soldier of the Civil War, and they made their home on a farm near the present town of Traer. About 1883, Mr. Thomas bought or traded for a hardware and farm implement business in the town of Traer, after which they rented the farm and made their residence there, where they lived the rest of their lives. Mr. Thomas died in 1912, and Mrs. Thomas died in 1916.

B. F. Thomas was born in Ohio and came to Iowa in 1856. He served four years in the Civil War, and after the war spent about twenty years at farming, after which he engaged in the hardware business in Traer for the rest of his life. He was a well educated man and at one time taught school. After the war he wrote a history of his regiment, the 14th Iowa Volunteers, (Infantry) having kept a diary during his four years' service.

The five living sons of Mr. and Mrs. Thomas are all active business and professional men. The oldest, John L., continues the hardware business; Arthur H. and B. Frank are engaged in the practice of law in Traer; Curtis H., is proprietor of a large green house in Traer, and the youngest son, William H., is a physician and surgeon at McGregor, Iowa.

Record of the B. F. and Sarah (Stoakes) Thomas Family

Names	Date of Birth	Date of Marriage	Residence or Death
Sarah E. Stoakes	March 17, 1838	Dec. 23, 1864	Died March 28, 1916
B. F. Thomas	March 6, 1837	Dec. 23, 1864	Died June 16, 1912

Children and Grand-Children of B. F. and Sarah (Stoakes) Thomas

John L. Thomas, born Dec. 20, 1865; married Oct. 16, 1890. Wife, Carrie Stoakes, born March 28, 1867. Residence, Traer, Iowa. Children: Ruth Thomas, born 1891; unmarried. Residence, Traer, Iowa. Paul Thomas, born 1894; married. Wife, Zenaide Kahler. Children: Virginia Thomas, born 1916; John Robert Thomas, born 1918. Residence, Traer, Iowa.

Philip Sheridan Thomas, born 1867; died 1867.

Arthur H. Thomas, born Sept. 10, 1869; married May 25, 1898. Wife, Christine Carpenter, born June 20, 1873. Daughter, Jean Thomas, born 1908; son, Roger A. Thomas, born 1909. Residence, Traer, Iowa.

Louis N. Thomas, born 1871; died 1891.

Curtis H. Thomas, born Feb. 27, 1874; married Aug. 1, 1900. Wife, Bertha King, born March 27, 1880. Children: Thesa Thomas, born 1902; Cassius Thomas, born 1907; Max Thomas, born 1909; Lewis Thomas, born 1916. Residence, Traer, Iowa.

B. Frank Thomas, born March 28, 1877; married Oct. 3, 1904. Wife, Grace Porterfield, born Oct. 29, 1882. Children: Dean P. Thomas, born 1905; Leonard C. Thomas, born 1907; Samuel K. Thomas, born 1909; Frinklin S. Thomas, born 1911; James N. Thomas, born 1919. Residence, Traer, Iowa.

William H. Thomas, born Aug. 10, 1879; married Nov. 4, 1903. Wife, Winnifred Fiete, born April 24, 1883. Daughter, Winnifred Thomas, born 1904. Residence, McGregor, Iowa.

THE GEORGE W. STOAKES BRANCH OF THE JOHN STOAKES, SR., FAMILY

George W. Stoakes, fifth and youngest son of John Stoakes, Sr., was born on the old homestead in Jefferson County, in 1843, and followed in the movings of his parents until they settled on the Tama County farm. In 1866 he married Alice Barbour, daughter of Dryden and Jane Barbour, who came from Ohio and settled in Tama County in 1856, soon after the Stoakes families located there. George W. and wife continued to live with his parents until their death, when he inherited the homestead of one-hundred and twenty acres, one and one-half miles northeast of Traer.   They were the parents of nine children, most of whom live in Tama and nearby counties.   Mr. and Mrs. Stoakes, although advanced in years, still live on the farm, town life having no lure for them. Both are well preserved and do much work.   George W. is the only surviving member of the John Stoakes Sr., family. The family have been noted for longevity, the father and mother and ten departed children have averaged near eighty-five years of age.

Record of the George W. and Alice (Barbour) Stoakes Family

Names	Date of Birth	Date of Marriage	Residence
George W. Stoakes	Sept. 14, 1843	Jan. 11, 1866	Traer, Iowa
Alice (Barbour) Stoakes	June 23, 1844	Jan. 11, 1866	Traer, Iowa

Children of George W. and Alice (Barbour) Stoakes

Martha Stoakes, born Feb. 22, 1867; married June 29, 1893. Husband, E. E. Campbell.   Residence, Cisno, Utah.

Dryden J. Stoakes, born May 10, 1868; married Dec. 18, 1889. Wife, Nellie B. Field.   Residence, Hardwick, Minn.

Henry E. Stoakes, born May 22, 1869; married Feb. 26, 1890. Wife, Ida S. Braden.   Residence, Goldfield, Iowa.

Rawlin G. Stoakes, born Dec. 14, 1870; married July 9, 1902. Wife, Westina Whannel.   Residence, Traer, Iowa.

Flavia Maude Stoakes, born Aug. 1, 1872; married Jan. 1, 1901. Husband, John B. Henry.   Residence, Goldfield, Iowa.

Alice Minerva Stoakes, born March 26, 1874;   married Dec. 23, 1898.   Husband, John Brown.   Residence,   Cedar Heights, Iowa.

Elizabeth Stoakes, born Jan. 29, 1877; died June 28, 1880.

Jay B. Stoakes, born Oct. 24, 1879; married Aug. 17, 1904.   Wife Mabel Townley.   Residence, Traer, Iowa.

Esther Stoakes, born Aug. 23, 1881; married Nov. 23, 1904. Died Dec. 8, 1916.   Husband, Robert Young.   Residence, Traer, Iowa.

Grand Children of George W. and Alice (Barbour) Stoakes

Children of E. E. and Martha (Stoakes) Campbell

Elvira Alice Campbell, born Oct. 3, 1894; married. Husband, John T. Sieber. Residence, Cisno, Utah.

Wesley Ernest Campbell, born Jan. 4, 1896; unmarried. Residence Cisno, Utah.

Esther Jeannette Campbell, born Aug. 7, 1899; unmarried. Residence Cisno, Utah.

Ethel Campbell, born Aug. 9, 1901; died Aug. 9, 1901.

Paul Early Campbell, born March 6, 1903. Residence, Cisno, Utah.

Dorris Martha Campbell, born April 15, 1905. Residence, Cisno, Utah.

Hugh George Campbell, born Sept. 19, 1907. Residence, Cisno, Utah.

Ruth Mabel Campbell, born March 6, 1910. Residence, Cisno, Utah.

Children of Dryden J. and Nellie B. (Field) Stoakes

Jay W. Stoakes, born Oct. 4, 1890; married Jan. 26, 1913. Wife, Margaret Weise. Children: Homer R. Stoakes, born Jan. 16, 1916; Horton K. Stoakes, born July 4, 1919. Residence, Hardwick, Minn.

George R. Stoakes, born Aug. 7, 1895; married June 4, 1915. Wife, Sylvia Beatty. Residence, Hardwick, Minn.

Mae Irene Stoakes, born Jan. 6, 1899; married Nov. 26, 1917. Husband, William Holling. Son: Russell W. Holling, born 1918. Residence, Hardwick, Minn.

Fay R. Stoakes, born Feb. 24, 1901; unmarried. Residence, Hardwick, Minn.

Ralph D. Stoakes, born May 7, 1909. Residence, Hardwick, Minn.

Children of Henry E. and Ida (Braden) Stoakes

Lawrence D. Stoakes, born Nov. 3, 1890; married. Died March 31, 1920. Wife, Ruth (Simmons) Stoakes, residence, Mason City, Iowa. Son: Richard L. Stoakes, born Nov. 5, 1917; died Jan. 25, 1919.

F. Kenneth Stoakes, born Sept. 23, 1899; married. Wife, Bernice Hill. Residence, Los Angeles, Cal.

Braden B. Stoakes, born May 4, 1902; unmarried. Residence, Goldfield, Iowa.

Carrie G. Stoakes, born March 28, 1906.   Residence, Goldfield, Iowa.

Children of Rawlin and Westina (Whannel) Stoakes

Evelyn Roberta Stoakes, born Dec. 22, 1905.

Jean Elizabeth Stoakes, born Jan. 2, 1910.

Westina Ruth Stoakes, born Nov. 24, 1913.

Residence, Traer, Iowa.

Children of John B. and Maude (Stoakes) Henry

Gretchen M. Henry, born March 10, 1905.   Residence, Goldfield, Iowa.

Chrissie Henry (step-daughter) born April 30, 1898; died June 17, 1917.

Children of John and Alice Minerva (Stoakes) Brown

Hobert Barbour Brown, born Nov. 1, 1902.

Jean Barbara Brown, born March 15, 1905.

Residence, Cedar Heights, Iowa.

Children of Jay B. and Mabel (Townley) Stoakes

Lucien Harry Stoakes, born Dec. 18, 1905.

Beth Stoakes, born Dec. 8, 1909.

Mark Dryden Stoakes, born May 10, 1914.

Residence, Traer, Iowa.

Children of Robert P. and Esther (Stoakes) Young

Alice Agnes Young, born Aug. 23, 1905.

Pauline Ruth Young, born Dec. 21, 1907.

Dorris Esther Young, born May 20, 1909.

Robert Peter Young, born Aug. 30, 1914.

Residence, Traer, Iowa.

RECORD OF THE WILLIAM STOAKES JR. (II) BRANCH OF THE STOAKES FAMILY

William Stoakes, Jr., was the oldest son of William Stoakes, Sr., who founded the Stoakes family in America, in 1797. He lived with his father and mother until their death in 1831, and inherited the original homestead. He and his wife, Keziah, lived on the place the rest of their lives, Mrs. Stoakes' death occuring in 1849, and Mr. Stoakes' in 1959.

Names	Date of Birth	Date of Marriage	Date of Death
William Stoakes, Jr.	May 17, 1789	Nov. 23, 1813	July 15, 1859
Keziah (Vantilburg) Stoakes	————————	Nov. 23, 1813	Oct. 30, 1849

Children of William Jr., (II) and Keziah (Vantilburg) Stoakes

Sarah Stoakes, born 1814; married March 15, 1838. Died March 1, 1882. Husband, Jas. A. Watt.

William Stoakes (II), born 1816. Unmarried. Died in 1852 of cholera in New Orleans, La.

Henry Stoakes Sr., (II) born 1818; married March 14, 1860. Died 1895. Wife, Letitia Caldwell; died May 16, 1889.

Jane Stoakes born 1820; unmarried. Died Oct. 20, 1899.

John Stoakes, Sr., (II) born Sept. 18, 1822; married Dec. 2, 1852. Died June 23, 1893. Wife, Susan Harrison. Died Nov. 20, 1893.

Isaac Stoakes, born 1824; unmarried. Died of cholera July 5, 1849, at Burlington, Ohio.

Benjamin Franklin Stoakes, born 1827; married Jan. 26, 1852. Died Oct. 6, 1909. Wife, Sarah Ann Mitchel. Died 1903.

Nancy Ellen Stoakes born 1830; married May 1, 1851. Died Oct. 20, 1851. Husband, John Harvison. Died in California.

Ann Eliza Stoakes, born 1835; married. Died Sept. 23, 1887. Husband, Charles Thomas Young.

DESCENDANTS OF WILLIAM JR., (II) AND KEZIAH (VANTILBURG) STOAKES

Record of the Jas. A. and Sarah (Stoakes) Watt Family

Sarah Stoakes, oldest daughter of William Jr., and Keziah (Vantilburg) Stoakes, was born Nov. 3, 1814, at the Knoxville home, and grew to womanhood there. In 1838 she married Jas.

A. Watt. Two children were born to them, Keziah Jane in 1838, and J. W., in 1840. In 1876 Keziah married Robert Hutchinson, and for several years lived in California. She lost her husband in 1888, and in 1889 returned to Ohio, where she has since resided. The son, J. W. Watt, went west to California, where he died Dec. 27, 1913, leaving many descendants. Mrs. Hutchinson is still living at Toronto, Jefferson County, Ohio, and is well preserved, both physically and mentally. Mrs. Watt died in 1882 and Mr. Watt in 1850.

Names	Date of Birth	Date of Marriage	Date of Death
Sarah Stoakes	Nov. 3, 1914	March 1, 1838	Died Mar. 1, 1882
Jas. A. Watt	——————	March 1, 1838	Died Oct. 20, 1850.

Children of Jas. A. and Sarah (Stoakes) Watt

Keziah Jane Watt, born 1838; married 1876. Residence, Toronto, Ohio. Husband, Robert Hutchinson. Died March 4, 1888. No children.

J. W. Watt, born March 5, 1840; married Feb. 3, 1868. Died Dec. 27, 1913. Wife, L. A. Caldwell, born Feb. 26, 1838. Died June 10, 1892.

Children of J. W. and L. A. (Caldwell) Watt

Fred W. Watt, born Oct. 20, 1875; married. Residence, Placerville, Cal. Wife, Susan A. Adams, born Jan. 24, 1882. Died Dec. 24, 1918. Children: Lynette Watt, born Oct. 8, 1905. Residence, Berkeley, Cal. William J. Watt, born Aug. 23, 1915. Residence, Placerville, Cal. Robert F. Watt, born May 23, 1918. Residence, Placerville, Cal.

RECORD OF THE HENRY, SR., (II) AND LETITIA (CALDWELL) STOAKES FAMILY

Henry Stoakes, the second son of William and Keziah Stoakes, was born at the old home in Ohio, in 1818, and spent most of his life in that locality. He was married in 1860 to Letitia Caldwell, and to them were born four children, three of whom died in infancy, and the fourth, Grant Stoakes, died in May, 1920, leaving a widow and three children, who live in Toronto, Ohio. Henry died of aparlysis, in 1895.

Names	Date of Birth	Date of Marriage	Date of Death
Henry Stoakes, Sr. (II)	Born in 1818	March 14, 1860	Died 1895
Letitia Caldwell	——————	March 14, 1860	Died, May 16, 1889

(Three children died in infancy)

Fourth Son of Henry and Letitia (Caldwell) Stoakes

Grant Stoakes, born ————; married 1900. Died in May, 1920.
Wife, Ellen Moran Stoakes. Residence, Toronto, Ohio.

Children of Grant and Ellen (Moran) Stoakes

Carrie Stoakes, born 1902.

Edward Stoakes, born 1905.

Jane Stoakes, born 1907.

Residence, Toronto, Ohio.

Adopted Son of Henry, Sr., and Letitia (Caldwell) Stoakes

Charles Stoakes, married. Wife, Maude Stoakes. Residence, Toronto, Ohio.

RECORD OF THE JOHN STOAKES, SR., (II) FAMILY

John Stoakes, Sr., (II), third son of William, Jr., and Keziah,
was born at the parental home in Jefferson County, Ohio, Sept. 20,
1822, and grew to manhood and spent his life in that locality. On
Dec. 2, 1852, he married Susan Harrison, and to this union were
born three children: Dr. William H. Stoakes, of Whittier, Cal.,
Frank Stoakes, who was a journalist, and when a boy of sixteen
revised and printed a pioneer history of the Morris-Miller and
Stoakes families. He went to California and died there in 1915.
He was born in 1860 and married Mary McFadden in 1886. They
had one son, Parke McFadden Stoakes, who was born in 1895, and
lives in Pittsburg, Pa. A third member of the family is Miss
Ella H. Stoakes, who was born in 1863. She has devoted her
life to educational work, and is now one of the faculty of Penn
College, Oskaloosa, Iowa. John Stoakes, the father, died June 23,
1893, and his wife on Nov. 20, 1893.

Descendants of the John Stoakes, Sr., (II) Family

Dr. William H. Stoakes, born Sept. 10, 1855; married Dec. 23,
1884. Wife, Jennie Myers. Residence, Whittier, Cal.

Frank Stoakes, born Jan. 1, 1860; married Oct. 27, 1886. Died in
California in 1915. Wife, Mary McFadden. Residence, California.

Ella H. Stoakes, born 1863; unmarried. Residence, Oskaloosa, Ia.

Children of Dr. William H. and Jennie (Myers) Stoakes

Dr. W. E. Stoakes, born Jan. 18, 1886; married Dec. 27, 1909. Wife, Nora West. Residence, Fort Douglas, New Mexico.

John H. Stoakes, born Aug. 6, 1890; married Oct. 23, 1813. Wife, Ruth Gualdin. Son, John Junior Stoakes, born September, 1914. Residence, Whittier, Cal.

Jean Stoakes, born Sept. 10, 1894; married Nov. 1917. First husband, Harry Bacon, died Oct. 1918. Second husband, Robert A. Osman; married Jan. 1920. Residence, Whittier, Cal.

Child of Frank and Mary (McFadden) Stoakes

Parke McFadden Stoakes, born June 25, 1895; married. Residence, Pittsburg, Pa.

RECORD OF THE LIFE OF WILLIAM STOAKES (II)

William Stoakes (II) oldest son of William Stoakes, Jr., and Keziah (Vantilburg) Stoakes, was born at the family home in Jefferson County, Ohio, in 1816, and lived in that locality the greater part of his life. He was never married and died in 1852 at New Orleans, La., of cholera.

RECORD OF THE LIFE OF ISAAC STOAKES

Isaac Stoakes, fourth son of William Stoakes, Jr., and Keziah (Vantilburg) Stoakes, was born at the family home in Jefferson County, Ohio, in 1824, and grew to manhood there. He never married, and died in 1849, at New Burlington, Lawrence County, Ohio, of cholera.

RECORD OF THE LIFE OF JANE STOAKES (II)

Jane Stoakes, second daughter of William, Jr., and Keziah (Vantilburg) Stoakes, was born Sept. 18, 1820, at the Knoxville home and spent her entire life there. She was never married, and died in 1899, just one hundred years from the first settlement of her grand-parents in that locality.

RECORD OF THE LIFE OF NANCY ANN STOAKES.

Nancy Ann Stoakes, third daughter of William, Jr., and Keziah (Vantilburg) Stoakes, was born at the family home in Jefferson County, Ohio, April 9, 1830, and grew to womanhood there. She was married in 1851 to John Harviston, but her wedded life was of short duration. She died in October of the same year. After her death, Mr. Harviston went to California, where he lived the remainder of his life.

RECORD OF THE CHARLES THOMAS AND ANN ELIZA (STOAKES) YOUNG FAMILY

Ann Eliza Stoakes, youngest daughter of William, Jr., and Keziah (Vantilburg) Stoakes, was born at the family home near Knoxville, Jefferson County, Ohio, in the year of 1835. She grew to womandhood there and married Charles Thomas Young. They had seven children, the first dying when quite young, and the other six are still living. Most of them live in or near Urichsville, and Dennison, Ohio. Mrs. Young died Sept. 23, 1887. One son, Charles William Young, lives at Logansport, Indiana. There are many descendants of the Stoakes-Young family living in and near Urichsville and Dennison, Ohio.

Charles Thomas and Ann Eliza (Stoakes) Young

Names	Date of Birth	Date of Marriage	Date of Death
Ann Eliza Stoakes	June 1, 1835.	————	Died Sept. 23, 1887.
Charles Thomas Young	————	————	————

Children of Charles Thomas and Ann Eliza (Stoakes) Young

Franklin Laomi Young, born June 9, 1867; died March 1, 1870.

Edwin Morris Young, born Nov. 1, 1868; married. Wife, Lizzie Rock. Residence, Dennison, Ohio.

Charles William Young, born June 23, 1870; married. Wife, Ella Buckey. Residence, Logansport, Indiana.

John Wesley Young, born Dec. 31, 1871; married. Wife, Anna Oberholzer. Residence, Dennison, Ohio.

Jessie Stoakes Young, born Nov. 13, 1873; married. Residence, Urichsville, Ohio. Husband, William Smith; dead.

Henry Stewart Young, born Oct. 18, 1876; married. Wife, Nora Haga. Residence, Urichsville, Ohio.

Addie Melissa Young, born Feb. 1879. Married. Husband, John Reese. Residence, Urichsville, Ohio.

Grand Children of Charles T. and Ann Eliza (Stoakes) Young

Children of Edwin Morris and Lizzie (Rock) Young

Ruth Edna Young, born Feb. 5, 1897; unmarried. Residence, Dennison, Ohio.
Anna May Young, born July 21, 1905; unmarried. Residence, Dennison, Ohio.

Children of Charles W. and Ella (Buckey) Young

Frank Young, born July 23, 1896; unmarried. Merchant Marine; New York City.
Mary Margaret Young, born Dec. 23, 1898. Died, May 27, 1901.
James Young, born Jan. 11, 1905. Residence, Logansport, Ind.
William Young, born Dec. 17, 1910. Residence, Logansport, Ind.

Children of John W. and Anna (Oberholzer) Young

Hazel Louise Young, born Oct. 5, 1902.
Marion Edith Young, born July 1, 1905.
Margaret Young, born Aug. 13, 1912.
Residence, Dennison, Ohio.

Children of William and Jessie (Young) Smith

Baby Smith, born July 1, 1895; died July 2, 1895.
William Donald Smith, born Feb. 11, 1897; married. Residence, Dennison, Ohio.

Child of Henry Stewart and Nora (Haga) Young

Mildred Young, born June 6, 1916; died June 7, 1916.

Children of John and Addie (Young) Reese

Jessie Hetty Reese, born Feb. 13, 1906.
Audley Leroy Reese, born Feb. 19, 1908.
Residence, Urichsville, Ohio.

Great Grandchild of Charles Thomas and Ann Eliza (Stoakes) Young

Son of William Donald Smith and Wife

John William Smith, born Nov. 14, 1919. Residence, Dennison, Ohio.

RECORD OF THE BENJAMIN FRANKLIN STOAKES FAMILY

Benjamin Franklin Stoakes, fifth son of William Jr., and Keziah Stoakes, was born in Ohio in 1827, and grew to manhood there, but spent his last years at Nevada City, California. In 1852 he married Sarah Ann Mitchell. To them were born five children, three of whom died in early childhood. The oldest daughter, Mrs. Flora V. (Stoakes) Rider, was born in Nevada City, California, in 1855, and was married to Charles Rider in 1903. Mr. Rider died in 1905. Mrs. Rider lives at San Leandro, California. Frank C. Stoakes, the youngest child of the B. F. Stoakes family, was born in 1862. He married in 1893 and raised a family of five children, all of whom are living. He died in 1917. Benjamin F. Stoakes died in 1911, and Mrs. Stoakes in 1903.

Name	Date of Birth	Married	Died
Benjamin F. Stoakes	Dec. 10, 1925,	Jan. 26, 1852	Oct. 5, 1911
Sarah A. Mitchell	Sept. 24, 1927.	Jan. 26, 1852	Aug. 23, 1903

Genealogy of the Benjamin Franklin Stoakes Family
Children of Benjamin Franklin and Sarah (Mitchell) Stoakes

Jennie Stoakes, born in Nevada City, Calif., 1853. Died in infancy.

Flora V. Stoakes, born March 31, 1855; married June 10, 1903. Husband, Chas. Rider, born Aug. 19, 1855, Sacramento, Calif., died April 5, 1905, at Oakland, Calif. Mrs. Rider resides at San Leandro, Calif.

Charles M. Stoakes, born in Nevada City, Calif., in 1856; died Dec. 10, 1860, at Nevada City, Calif.

Belle S. Stoakes, born in Nevada City, Calif., 1858; died Jan. 10, 1861, at Nevada City, Calif.

Frank C. Stoakes, born Oct. 9, 1862; married Aug. 23, 1893; died Aug. 20, 1917, at San Leandro, Calif. Wife, Minnie Olcesr; residence San Leandro, Calif.

Children of Frank C. and Minnie O. Stoakes

Dr. Frank Olcesr Stoakes, born July 16, 1894, at Oakland, Calif.; married May 4, 1921. Wife, Mary Elizabeth Eickholt; residence, Rochester, Calif.

Ethel A. Stoakes, born Jan. 21, 1896, at Oakland, Calif.; residence, San Leandro, Calif.

Lester B. Stoakes, born Sept. 2, 1897, at Oakland, Calif.; residence, Bakersfield, Calif.

Milton Stoakes, born July 3, 1902, at Oakland, Calif.; residence, San Leandro, Calif.

Marguerite Stoakes, born July 15, 1904, San Leandro, Calif.; residence, San Leandro, Calif.

INDEX TO NAMES USED IN THE STOAKES FAMILY HISTORY AND GENEALOGY